# Michael Palin

Sir Michael Edward Palin KCMG CBE FRGS FRSGS FRSL, born on May 5, 1943, in England, is a multifaceted individual renowned for his contributions as an actor, comedian, writer, and television presenter. His illustrious career spans decades and encompasses achievements in various fields.

Palin's early foray into television included work on programs such as the Ken Dodd Show, The Frost Report, and Do Not Adjust Your Set. However, he truly gained widespread recognition as a member of the legendary Monty Python comedy group, joining forces with John Cleese, Eric Idle, Terry Gilliam, Terry Jones, and Graham Chapman for the groundbreaking Monty Python's Flying Circus (1969–1974). His participation in some of the most iconic Python sketches, including "Argument Clinic," "Dead Parrot sketch," "The Lumberjack Song," "The Spanish Inquisition," "Bicycle Repair Man," and "The Fish-Slapping Dance," solidified his status as a comedic talent.

Palin's collaboration with Terry Jones extended beyond Monty Python, leading to the co-writing of Ripping Yarns. Further establishing his creative prowess, Palin co-wrote and starred in cinematic classics such as Monty Python and the Holy Grail (1975), Life of Brian (1979), and The Meaning of Life (1983).

Beyond the realm of comedy, Palin showcased his acting versatility in A Fish Called Wanda (1988), earning the BAFTA Award for Best Actor in a Supporting Role. Notable contributions to film also include Jabberwocky (1977), Time Bandits (1981), The Missionary (1982), A Private Function (1984), Brazil (1985), Fierce Creatures (1997), and The Death of Stalin (2017).

From 1980 onward, Palin embarked on a new chapter in his career, becoming a prolific travel documentarian. His captivating television travel documentaries, broadcast on the BBC, have taken audiences on journeys to diverse corners of the globe, including the North and South Poles, the Sahara, the Himalayas, Eastern Europe, and Brazil. Notably, in 2018, he ventured into the enigmatic North Korea, documenting his experiences in a series broadcast on Channel 5.

In addition to his creative endeavors, Palin served as the President of the Royal Geographical Society from 2009 to 2012, further demonstrating his commitment to exploration and understanding of the world.

His remarkable career, marked by accolades such as the BAFTA Fellowship in 2013 and knighthood bestowed by Queen Elizabeth II in 2019, attests to the enduring impact of Sir Michael Palin on the realms of comedy, film, literature, and exploration.

Palin's post-Monty Python career has been characterized by a remarkable fusion of entertainment and exploration. His transition from comedy to travel documentaries showcased his insatiable curiosity and passion for discovering the diverse cultures and landscapes of the world.

As a travel writer and presenter, Palin has left an indelible mark on the genre. His journeys have not only entertained but also enlightened audiences, offering a unique blend of humor, cultural insight, and genuine curiosity. From the frozen expanses of the North and South Poles to the arid landscapes of the Sahara and the majestic peaks of the Himalayas, Palin's travels have been both visually stunning and intellectually enriching.

One of his notable achievements was the documentation of his visit to North Korea in 2018, providing a rare glimpse into the isolated country. This series underscored Palin's commitment to traversing both well-trodden and less-explored paths, offering viewers a nuanced understanding of the world's complexities.

Beyond his on-screen adventures, Palin's role as the President of the Royal Geographical Society from 2009 to 2012 reflected his dedication to the advancement of geographic knowledge and exploration. His influence extended beyond the entertainment industry, contributing to the promotion of geographical understanding and appreciation.

In addition to his televised explorations, Palin is a widely recognized and respected author. His travelogues, including "Around the World in 80 Days" and "Pole to Pole," have captured the essence of his journeys in written form, allowing readers to embark on vicarious adventures through his vivid narratives.

The enduring legacy of Sir Michael Palin is not merely confined to the laughter he elicited through Monty Python's comedic genius or the breathtaking landscapes he unveiled in his travel documentaries. It is a testament to the boundless curiosity and versatility that have defined his career. From the absurdity of Python sketches to the awe-inspiring vistas of far-flung corners of the globe, Palin's contributions have transcended entertainment, leaving an indelible mark on the cultural and geographical tapestry of our world. Sir Michael Palin's life and work stand as a testament to the profound impact that one individual can have when armed with humor, intellect, and an unwavering commitment to exploration.

Early Life and Education:

Sir Michael Edward Palin was born on May 5, 1943, in Ranmoor, Sheffield, as the second child and only son of Edward Moreton Palin and Mary Rachel Lockhart (née Ovey). Edward Palin, his father, was a Cambridge-educated engineer employed by a steel firm, while his maternal grandfather, Lieutenant-Colonel Richard Lockhart Ovey, DSO, held the position of High Sheriff of Oxfordshire in 1927.

Palin's educational journey began at Birkdale and later continued at Shrewsbury School. Despite a significant age gap, he shared a close bond with his sister Angela until her tragic suicide in 1987. The impact of this loss would shape Palin's life profoundly.

Coming from a background of English and Irish Catholic heritage, Palin discovered ancestral roots in Letterkenny, County Donegal. His great-grandmother's escape from the Irish Famine and subsequent adoption by a wealthy English family added layers to his diverse heritage.

Palin's interest in acting surfaced at a young age. At the age of five, he took on the role of Martha Cratchit in a school performance of "A Christmas Carol" at Birkdale. This early experience kindled a passion for the stage. By the age of 10, he was already showcasing his comedic talent, delivering a monologue and reading a Shakespeare play while assuming all the roles for his mother.

In 1962, after completing his education at Shrewsbury, Palin pursued a degree in modern history at Brasenose College, Oxford. It was during this time that he teamed up with fellow student Robert Hewison to perform and write comedy material at a university Christmas party. This collaboration caught the attention of Terry Jones, another Oxford student, leading to the formation of a creative partnership.

Palin's involvement with the Brightside and Carbrook Co-operative Society Players marked his initial foray into the world of acting, earning him recognition with an acting award at a Co-op drama festival. Concurrently, he contributed to the Oxford Revue, known as the Et ceteras, showcasing his comedic talents alongside Terry Jones.

This early period of Palin's life not only laid the foundation for his future in comedy and acting but also hinted at the diverse and expansive career that would unfold in the years to come.

Upon completing his university education in 1965, Michael Palin embarked on the early stages of his career, demonstrating his versatility as a presenter and comedy writer. His journey in the entertainment industry began with a role as a presenter on the comedy pop show "Now!" for Television Wales and the West.

During this time, Palin's creative path intertwined with that of Terry Jones, who had contacted him to collaborate on writing a theatrical documentary about the history of sex. Although this particular project was eventually abandoned, it laid the foundation for a lasting creative partnership between Palin and Jones. The duo began crafting comedy for various BBC programs, including "The Ken Dodd Show," "The Billy Cotton Bandshow," and "The Illustrated Weekly Hudd." They also contributed lyrics to Barry Booth's album titled "Diversions."

Their collaboration expanded further as part of the writing team for "The Frost Report," a pivotal moment as it marked the first time that all the British members of Monty Python, excluding Terry Gilliam, worked together. During the show's run, Palin and Jones contributed material to other productions such as "The Late Show" and "A Series of Birds," starring John Bird. It was during "A Series of Birds" that Palin and Jones delved into writing narrative, a departure from the short sketches they were accustomed to creating.

Post-"The Frost Report," Palin and Jones continued their collaboration, working as both actors and writers on shows like "Twice a Fortnight" with Graeme Garden, Bill Oddie, and Jonathan Lynn. They also contributed to the children's comedy show "Do Not Adjust Your Set," featuring Eric Idle and David Jason. This show included musical numbers by the Bonzo Dog Doo-Dah Band, including Neil Innes, who would later collaborate with Monty Python on musical projects. The animations for "Do Not Adjust Your Set" were crafted by Terry Gilliam.

Palin's talent and reputation led to an invitation from John Cleese to join the cast of "How to Irritate People," alongside Graham Chapman and Tim Brooke-Taylor. This collaboration, sans Jones, showcased Palin's ability to seamlessly integrate into various comedic ensembles.

The Palin/Jones team eventually reunited for "The Complete and Utter History of Britain," solidifying their status as a dynamic creative duo in the comedy landscape. This period of Palin's early career laid the groundwork for the groundbreaking work that would follow with Monty Python and beyond.

Following their success on "The Complete and Utter History of Britain," the Palin/Jones team continued to make significant contributions to the world of comedy. Their collaborative efforts led them to new opportunities in both writing and performing, showcasing their comedic prowess and innovative approach to humor.

A notable venture was the iconic "Monty Python's Flying Circus," which brought together the comedic talents of John Cleese, Eric Idle, Terry Gilliam, Terry Jones, Graham Chapman, and Michael Palin. This groundbreaking television series, which ran from 1969 to 1974, became a cultural phenomenon, known for its surreal sketches, irreverent humor, and absurd characters. Palin's versatility as a performer shone through in memorable sketches such as "Argument Clinic," "Dead Parrot sketch," "The Lumberjack Song," and "The Fish-Slapping Dance."

Palin's collaborative spirit extended beyond Monty Python, as he joined forces with Terry Jones to co-write "Ripping Yarns," a television series that showcased their narrative storytelling abilities. This endeavor highlighted their versatility beyond the sketch comedy format, demonstrating a mastery of longer-form storytelling.

The creative synergy between Palin and Jones reached new heights with their work on Monty Python's cinematic ventures, including "Monty Python and the Holy Grail" (1975), "Life of Brian" (1979), and "The Meaning of Life" (1983). These films further solidified the legacy of Monty Python, captivating audiences with their unique blend of wit, satire, and absurdity.

Palin's individual achievements in film extended beyond Monty Python, with his standout performance in "A Fish Called Wanda" (1988) earning him the BAFTA Award for Best Actor in a Supporting Role. His filmography also includes notable works such as "Jabberwocky" (1977), "Time Bandits" (1981), "Brazil" (1985), and "The Death of Stalin" (2017), showcasing his range as an actor in various genres.

Parallel to his success in the world of comedy and film, Palin embarked on a new chapter as a travel documentarian. Starting in 1980, he became widely recognized for his engaging travel documentaries that took viewers on journeys across the globe. From the frozen landscapes of the North and South Poles to the vibrant cultures of Eastern Europe and the mystique of North Korea, Palin's travels not only entertained but also educated audiences about the diverse facets of our world.

In recognition of his outstanding contributions, Palin was honored with the BAFTA Fellowship in 2013, a testament to his enduring impact on the world of entertainment. Subsequently, in 2019, Queen Elizabeth II knighted him, further acknowledging his significant achievements in the fields of comedy, film, and television.

Sir Michael Palin's journey, marked by innovation, humor, and a relentless curiosity about the world, continues to inspire and entertain audiences globally. His legacy extends far beyond the realms of comedy, encompassing the spirit of exploration and the boundless possibilities of creative collaboration.

Monty Python, the iconic comedy troupe, stands as one of the most influential and groundbreaking collectives in the history of humor. Sir Michael Palin played a pivotal role in the formation and success of Monty Python's Flying Circus, contributing his wit, versatility, and comedic talent to create a comedic legacy that has endured for decades.

The origins of Monty Python trace back to a fortuitous collaboration between Palin and John Cleese. Cleese, having been offered a show by the BBC, sought a creative partner, and his desire to work with Palin became a catalyst for the formation of Monty Python. Simultaneously, Palin, along with Terry Jones, Eric Idle, and Terry Gilliam, had achieved success with "Do Not Adjust Your Set" and was offered their own series. The convergence of these circumstances brought together the diverse talents that would constitute the Monty Python troupe.

Palin's contributions to Monty Python were characterized by a wide range of roles, showcasing his ability to embody characters with manic enthusiasm, unflappable calmness, and socially inept charm. From the iconic lumberjack in "The Lumberjack Song" to the dead parrot vendor and the Cheese Shop proprietor, Palin's performances added depth and humor to the sketches. As a straight man, he often served as a foil to the escalating madness of characters portrayed by Cleese.

His versatility was evident in his portrayal of timid characters like Arthur Putey, the man who stoically observes a marriage counselor's unconventional session. Palin's role as Mr. Anchovy, a chartered accountant aspiring to be a lion tamer, further showcased his ability to bring humor to a diverse array of characters. Additionally, his recurring appearances as the "It's" man and the notorious Gumby character, known for their moronic views expressed with force, became beloved elements of the show.

Palin's creative partnership with Terry Jones flourished, resulting in co-written sketches such as the legendary "Spanish Inquisition sketch," famous for the catchphrase "Nobody expects the Spanish Inquisition!" Their collaboration extended to musical compositions, with hits like "The Lumberjack Song," "Every Sperm Is Sacred," and "Spam." Palin also ventured into solo musical compositions, including the witty "Decomposing Composers" and the humorous ode to Finland.

Monty Python's Flying Circus revolutionized comedy, challenging conventions and leaving an indelible mark on the genre. Michael Palin's comedic genius and collaborative spirit played a crucial role in the success of the troupe, contributing to its enduring legacy and cultural significance.

In the post-Monty Python era, spanning from 1974 to 1996, Michael Palin continued to demonstrate his creative versatility, engaging in a range of projects that showcased his talent as both a writer and actor.

In 1971, Palin collaborated with Hugh Leonard and Terence Feely to co-write the film "Percy." This unconventional comedy delves into the theme of a penis transplant, showcasing Palin's willingness to explore boundary-pushing and irreverent subject matter.

Following the conclusion of the Monty Python television series in 1974, Palin joined forces with Terry Jones to create "Ripping Yarns," a television comedy series that aired intermittently over three years starting in 1976. Building on their previous collaboration on the play "Secrets" from the BBC series "Black and Blue" in 1973, Palin and Jones continued to showcase their narrative storytelling skills in this series.

Palin took on the lead role of the peasant Dennis in Terry Gilliam's 1977 film "Jabberwocky." Notably, Palin had previously played a cameo role as "Dennis the Peasant" in the Monty Python film "Monty Python and the Holy Grail," also directed by Gilliam.

In 1978, Palin appeared in "All You Need Is Cash" as Eric Manchester, a character based on Derek Taylor, the press agent for the Rutles. His collaborative efforts with Gilliam continued in 1980 with the co-writing of "Time Bandits," in which Palin also played a role.

In 1982, Palin wrote and starred in "The Missionary," co-starring with Maggie Smith. The film follows the story of Reverend Charles Fortescue, who is recalled from Africa to aid prostitutes. Palin and Smith collaborated again in the 1984 comedy film "A Private Function."

Continuing his creative partnership with Terry Gilliam, Palin appeared in the acclaimed film "Brazil" in 1984. His role in "A Fish Called Wanda" (1988), a comedy co-written and co-starring John Cleese, earned him the BAFTA Award for Best Actor in a Supporting Role.

Palin's cinematic journey also led him to collaborate on "Fierce Creatures," a reunion of the main cast from "A Fish Called Wanda." Following the completion of filming for "Fierce Creatures," Palin embarked on a travel journey for a BBC documentary. Upon his return a year later, he discovered that the end of "Fierce Creatures" had not resonated well in test screenings and needed to be reshot.

This period in Palin's career exemplifies his commitment to diverse and challenging projects, showcasing his ability to excel in both comedic and dramatic roles on both the big and small screens.

From 1996 onward, Michael Palin's career continued to evolve, showcasing his versatility as both an actor and a presenter. Here's a glimpse into his endeavors during this period:

After "Fierce Creatures" and a small role in Terry Jones's film adaptation of "The Wind in the Willows," there was a two-decade gap before Palin's next film role. In 2017, he portrayed Soviet politician Vyacheslav Molotov in the satirical black comedy "The Death of Stalin." Palin also made an appearance alongside John Cleese in Cleese's documentary, "The Human Face." Notably, Palin was initially cast in a supporting role in the romantic comedy "You've Got Mail," but his part was ultimately cut.

Palin ventured into serious drama with the 1991 film "American Friends," a project he wrote based on a real event in his great-grandfather's life. In the same year, he played the role of a headmaster in Alan Bleasdale's Channel 4 drama series "GBH." Additionally, Palin narrated the English language audiobook version of Roald Dahl's "Esio Trot" in 1994.

In 1997, Palin made a small cameo appearance in the Australian soap opera "Home and Away," playing an English surfer with a fear of sharks. This cameo was part of the Full Circle series, which included a segment about the filming of his role.

Palin's involvement in various projects continued in the following years. In 2013, he appeared in the First World War drama "The Wipers Times," written by Ian Hislop and Nick Newman. The announcement at the Cannes Film Festival in 2016 that Palin would star alongside Adam Driver in Terry Gilliam's "The Man Who Killed Don Quixote" didn't come to fruition as he had to drop out due to financial issues.

A notable addition to Palin's documentary work was the two-part documentary "Michael Palin in North Korea," which aired on Channel 5 in the UK and National Geographic in the United States in 2018. The documentary provided a rare glimpse into the isolated country.

In July 2019, Palin performed a one-man stage show at the Torch Theatre in Wales, focusing on the loss of HMS Erebus during the third Franklin expedition. This stage show was based on his book "Erebus: The Story of a Ship."

Michael Palin's career post-1996 showcases his continued commitment to diverse and meaningful projects, spanning film, television, documentary work, and live performances.

Michael Palin's exploration of the world through travel documentaries has been a significant part of his career, showcasing not only his adventurous spirit but also his storytelling prowess. Here is an overview of his travel documentaries from 1980 to the present:

Great Railway Journeys of the World (1980):

Episode: "Confessions of a Trainspotter"
Palin humorously reminisces about his childhood hobby of train spotting as he travels throughout the UK by train, from London to the Kyle of Lochalsh.
Travel Series for the BBC (1989-2012):

After Alan Whicker and Miles Kington turned down presenting the first travel series, Palin had the opportunity to host his first and subsequent travel shows.
Notable series include:
"Around the World in 80 Days with Michael Palin" (1988/1989)
"Pole to Pole with Michael Palin" (1991/1992)
"Full Circle with Michael Palin" (1995/1996)
"Michael Palin's Hemingway Adventure" (1999)
"Sahara with Michael Palin" (2001/2002)
"Himalaya with Michael Palin" (2003/2004)
"Michael Palin's New Europe" (2006/2007)
"Brazil with Michael Palin" (2012)

Channel 5 Travel Documentaries (2018-2022):

In 2018, Palin presented "Michael Palin in North Korea" for Channel 5, offering a rare glimpse into the isolated country.
In 2022, he presented "Michael Palin: Into Iraq" for Channel 5.
Photography Books:

For four of the trips, Basil Pao, the stills photographer on the team, created large coffee-table style photography books, each with an introduction written by Palin.
The "Palin Effect":

Palin's travel programs are credited with the "Palin effect," where areas he visited become popular tourist attractions. For example, the surge in tourists interested in Peru after Palin's visit to Machu Picchu.
Favourite Place:

In a 2006 survey by The Observer, Palin named Peru's Pongo de Mainique (canyon below Machu Picchu) as his "favourite place in the world."
Around the World in 80 Days:

Palin notes in his book that the final leg of his journey could have taken him through the Clapham Junction rail crash, but they arrived ahead of schedule and caught an earlier train.

Michael Palin's exploration of art and history through documentary programs has added another dimension to his diverse body of work. Here's an overview of his ventures into the realms of art and history:

Documentaries on Artists:

"Palin on Redpath" (1997): Explored the work of Scottish painter Anne Redpath.
"The Bright Side of Life" (2000): Focused on the Scottish Colourists, a group of artists renowned for their use of color.
"Michael Palin and the Ladies Who Loved Matisse" (2004): Explored the life and work of French artist Henri Matisse.
"Michael Palin and the Mystery of Hammershøi" (2005): Investigated the art of Danish painter Vilhelm Hammershøi.
"Michael Palin in Wyeth World" (2013): Traveled to the United States, specifically Maine and Pennsylvania, to delve into the life and art of American painter Andrew Wyeth and the individuals who inspired his paintings.
DVD Release:

The DVD titled "Michael Palin on Art" includes documentaries on Anne Redpath, the Scottish Colourists, and the mystery of Hammershøi.
First World War Documentary (2008):

In November 2008, Palin presented a documentary for the BBC's Timewatch series titled "The Last Day of World War One." This program explored the events of Armistice Day, 11 November 1918, and the tragic loss of soldiers' lives in battle after the war had officially ended. Palin filmed on the battlefields of Northern France and Belgium for this project.

Michael Palin's personal life is marked by a long and enduring marriage, a close-knit family, and various personal interests. Here are some key aspects of his personal life:

Marriage:

In 1966, Palin married Helen Gibbins, whom he had first met in 1959 while on holiday in Southwold, Suffolk. This meeting was later fictionalized in Palin's teleplay for the 1987 BBC television drama "East of Ipswich."
The marriage lasted for an impressive 57 years until Helen's passing on May 2, 2023, due to kidney failure.
Children and Grandchildren:

Michael and Helen Palin have three children: Thomas (born 1969), William (born 1970), and Rachel (born 1975).
Rachel Palin is a BBC TV director, known for her work on "MasterChef: The Professionals."
William Palin serves as the Director of Conservation at the Old Royal Naval College in Greenwich, London. He oversaw the restoration of the Painted Hall in 2018–19.
There are four grandchildren in the Palin family.
Other Family Ties:

William Palin made a brief appearance as a baby in the film "Monty Python and the Holy Grail," credited as "Sir Not-appearing-in-this-film."
Jeremy Herbert, a theatre designer, is Michael Palin's nephew.
Religious Belief:

Michael Palin describes his religious belief as "agnostic with doubts," reflecting a stance of uncertainty or skepticism regarding religious doctrines.
Residence:

Palin has lived in Gospel Oak, London, since the 1960s.

Michael Palin has been actively involved in various advocacy and charity efforts, demonstrating a commitment to causes related to sustainable transport, the environment, and the well-being of indigenous communities. Here are some instances of his activism and charity work:

Campaign for Better Transport:

Palin has been a staunch supporter of the Campaign for Better Transport, particularly in campaigns related to sustainable transport in urban areas.
He has served as the president of the campaign since 1986.
Fair Fares Now Campaign:

On 2 January 2011, Michael Palin became the first person to sign the UK-based Campaign for Better Transport's Fair Fares Now campaign, advocating for fair and reasonable transportation fares.
Support for the BBC:

In July 2015, Palin signed an open letter and gave an interview to express support for "a strong BBC at the centre of British life" during a period when the government was reviewing the corporation's size and activities.
Advocacy for Indigenous Rights:

In July 2010, Palin voiced his support for the Dongria Kondh tribe of India, who were resisting mining on their land by the company Vedanta Resources.
Palin's message highlighted the challenges faced by the tribe and their sustainable practices, emphasizing their desire to continue living in their ancestral villages.

Here is a summary of Michael Palin's filmography:

Film:

1971: "And Now for Something Completely Different" (Various roles, also writer)
1975: "Monty Python and the Holy Grail" (Sir Galahad the Pure, Leader of the Knights Who Say Ni, Various roles)
1977: "Jabberwocky" (Dennis Cooper)
1978: "All You Need Is Cash" (Eric Manchester/Lawyer)
1979: "Monty Python's Life of Brian" (Pontius Pilate, Various roles, also writer)
1981: "Time Bandits" (Vincent)
1982: "Monty Python Live at the Hollywood Bowl" (Various roles)
1982: "The Missionary" (The Reverend Charles Fortescue, also writer and producer)
1983: "Monty Python's The Meaning of Life" (Various roles, also writer)
1983: "The Crimson Permanent Assurance" (Workman, Short film)
1984: "A Private Function" (Gilbert Chilvers)
1985: "Brazil" (Jack Lint)
1987: "The Grand Knockout Tournament" (Himself, Television special)
1988: "A Fish Called Wanda" (Ken Pile)
1991: "American Friends" (Reverend Francis Ashby, also writer)
1996: "The Wind in the Willows" (The Sun, Voice only)
1997: "Fierce Creatures" (Adrian 'Bugsy' Malone)
2010: "Not the Messiah" (Mrs. Betty Palin/Pontius Pilate/Bevis)
2011: "Arthur Christmas" (Ernie Clicker, Voice only)
2012: "A Liar's Autobiography: The Untrue Story of Monty Python's Graham Chapman" (Various roles)
2014: "Monty Python Live" (Also writer)
2015: "Absolutely Anything" (Kindly Alien, Voice only)
2017: "The Death of Stalin" (Vyacheslav Molotov)

Here is a list of Michael Palin's contributions to television, radio, and literature:

Television:

Now! (October 1965 – middle 1966)
The Ken Dodd Show
Billy Cotton Bandshow
The Illustrated Weekly Hudd
The Frost Report (10 March 1966 – 29 June 1967)
The Late Show (15 October 1966 – 1 April 1967)
A Series of Bird's (1967) (3 October 1967 – 21 November 1967 screenwriter (guest stars)
Twice a Fortnight (21 October 1967 – 23 December 1967)
Do Not Adjust Your Set (26 December 1967 – 14 May 1969)
Broaden Your Mind (1968)
How to Irritate People (1968)
Marty (1968)
The Complete and Utter History of Britain (1969)
Monty Python's Flying Circus (5 October 1969 – 5 December 1974)
Three Men in a Boat (1975)
Saturday Night Live (Hosted on various dates)
Ripping Yarns (1976–1979)
Great Railway Journeys of the World, episode title "Confessions of a Trainspotter" (1980)
East of Ipswich (1987) (writer)

Around the World in 80 Days with Michael Palin (1989)
GBH (1991)
Pole to Pole with Michael Palin (1992)
Tracey Ullman: A Class Act (1993)
Great Railway Journeys, episode title "Derry to Kerry" (1994)
The Wind in the Willows (1995)
The Willows in Winter (1996)
Full Circle with Michael Palin (1997)
Palin on Redpath (1997)
Monty Python Live at Aspen (1998)
Michael Palin's Hemingway Adventure (1999)
Michael Palin On... The Colourists (2000)
Sahara with Michael Palin (2002)
Life on Air (2002)
Himalaya with Michael Palin (2004)
Michael Palin and the Ladies Who Loved Matisse (2004)
Michael Palin and the Mystery of Hammershøi (2005)
Michael Palin's New Europe (2007)
Robbie the Reindeer – Close Encounters of the Herd Kind (2007 – Gariiiiiii/Gary)
Around the World in 20 Years (30 December 2008)
Brazil with Michael Palin (2012)
The Wipers Times (2013)
Michael Palin in Wyeth's World (2013)

Remember Me (2014)
Clangers (2015 – narrator)
Michael Palin's Quest for Artemisia (2015)
Vanity Fair (William Makepeace Thakery, 2018)
Michael Palin in North Korea (2018)
Worzel Gummidge: the Green Man (2019)
The Simpsons: Museum Curator (2020)
Michael Palin: Travels of a Lifetime (2020)
Michael Palin's Himalaya: Journey of a Lifetime (2020)
Michael Palin: Into Iraq (2022)
Radio:

The Weekend (2017, adapted from his 1994 stage play)
*John Finnemore's Double Acts – "The Wroxton Box" (Series 2, Episode 6; 2017)
*Torchwood: Tropical Beach Sounds and Other Relaxing Seascapes #4 (April 2020)

Bibliography:
Travel Books:

Around the World in 80 Days (1989)
Pole to Pole (1992)
Full Circle (1997)
Michael Palin's Hemingway Adventure (1999)
Sahara (2002)
Himalaya (2004)
New Europe (2007)
Brazil (2012)
North Korea Journal (2019)
Into Iraq (2022)
All but the latest two of his travel books can be read with no charge, complete and unabridged, on Palin's Travels website.

Here is a list of Michael Palin's contributions to autobiography, diaries, fiction, non-fiction, children's books, and plays:

Autobiography (Contributor):

The Pythons Autobiography by The Pythons (2003) ISBN 0-7528-5293-0
Diaries:

Diaries 1969–1979: The Python Years (2006) ISBN 978-0-297-84436-5
Diaries 1980–1988: Halfway to Hollywood – The Film Years (2009) ISBN 978-0-297-84440-2
Diaries 1988–1998: Travelling to Work (2014) ISBN 978-0-297-84441-9
Diaries 1999–2015: TBC (Announced for 2024) ISBN 978-1-474-61275-3
Fiction:

Bert Fegg's Nasty Book for Boys and Girls with Terry Jones, illus Martin Honeysett, Frank Bellamy et al. (1974) ISBN 0-413-32740-X
Dr Fegg's Encyclopaedia of All World Knowledge (1984) (expanded reprint of the above, with Terry Jones and Martin Honeysett) ISBN 0-87226-005-4
Hemingway's Chair (1995) ISBN 0-7493-1930-5
The Truth (2012) ISBN 978-0297860211

Non-fiction:

Erebus: The Story of a Ship (2018, UK) ISBN 978-1847948120
Erebus: One Ship, Two Epic Voyages, and the Greatest Naval Mystery of All Time (2018, US/Canada) ISBN 978-1771644419
Great-Uncle Harry: A Tale of War and Empire (2023) ISBN 978-1039001985
Children's Books:

Small Harry and the Toothache Pills (1982) ISBN 0-416-23690-1
Limericks or The Limerick Book (1985) ISBN 0-09-161540-2
Cyril and the House of Commons (1986) ISBN 1-85145-078-5
Cyril and the Dinner Party (1986) ISBN 1-85145-069-6
The Mirrorstone with Alan Lee and Richard Seymour (1986) ISBN 0-224-02408-6
Plays:

The Weekend (1994) ISBN 0-413-68940-9

Awards, Honours, and Legacy (continued):

Palin played a key role in establishing the Michael Palin Centre for Stammering Children in 1993.

In 1993, each member of Monty Python had an asteroid named after them, and Palin's is Asteroid 9621 Michaelpalin.

Inside the Globe Theatre, a commemorative stone was placed in 2003 to mark donors to the theatre, and Palin has his own stone, although it is misspelled as "Michael Pallin," a playful misspelling insisted upon by John Cleese.

Two British trains have been named after Palin. In 2002, Virgin Trains' high-speed Super Voyager train number 221130 was named Michael Palin, and National Express East Anglia named a British Rail Class 153 (unit number 153335) after him.

In 2008, Palin received the James Joyce Award of the Literary and Historical Society in Dublin.

For his contributions to the promotion of geography, Palin was awarded the Livingstone Medal of the Royal Scottish Geographical Society in March 2009, along with a Fellowship of this Society (FRGS).

In June 2013, Palin received a gold medal for achievements in geography from the Royal Canadian Geographical Society.

He was elected President of the Royal Geographical Society for a three-year term in June 2009.

Often referred to as "Britain's Nicest Man," Palin was named the greatest Yorkshireman ever in a 2018 poll for Yorkshire Day.

In September 2013, Moorlands School in Leeds named one of their school houses "Palin" in his honour.

The University of St Andrews awarded Palin an honorary Doctor of Science degree in June 2017 for his contribution to the public's understanding of contemporary geography.

In October 2018, the Royal Canadian Geographical Society awarded Palin the first Louie Kamookak Medal for advances in geography.

Palin was appointed a Commander of the Order of the British Empire (CBE) in the 2000 New Year Honours.

In the 2019 New Year Honours, Palin was appointed a Knight Commander of the Order of St Michael and St George (KCMG) for "services to travel, culture, and geography." He is the only member of the Monty Python team to receive a knighthood.

In 2017, the British Library acquired Palin's archive, consisting of project files related to his work, notebooks, and personal diaries, covering his contributions to Monty Python, TV work, and children's and humorous books.

BAFTA Awards:

1984:

Nominated – BAFTA Award for "Best Original Song" (the award was discontinued after the 1985 ceremonies) for "Every Sperm is Sacred" from The Meaning of Life (shared with André Jacquemin, Dave Howman, and Terry Jones).
1989:

Won – BAFTA Award for Best Actor in a Supporting Role for A Fish Called Wanda (as Ken Pile).
1992:

Nominated – British Academy Television Award for Best Actor for GBH.
2005:

Won – BAFTA Special Award.
2009:

Won – BAFTA Special Award as part of the Monty Python team for outstanding contribution to film and television.
2013:

Won – BAFTA Academy Fellowship Award.
Other Awards:

2011:

Awarded the Aardman Slapstick Visual Comedy Legend award for "significant contributions made to the world of comedy."
2020:

National Television Awards Special Recognition Award.

Printed in Great Britain
by Amazon

42358667R00020

"MICHAEL PALIN: A LIFE OF WIT, WANDERLUST, AND WHIMSY" IS A CAPTIVATING BIOGRAPHY THAT DELVES INTO THE EXTRAORDINARY LIFE AND MULTIFACETED CAREER OF ONE OF BRITAIN'S MOST BELOVED ENTERTAINERS. FROM HIS EARLY DAYS AS A COMEDIAN AND WRITER WITH THE ICONIC MONTY PYTHON TROUPE TO HIS GLOBETROTTING ADVENTURES AS A TRAVEL DOCUMENTARIAN, PALIN'S JOURNEY IS RICH WITH HUMOR, CURIOSITY, AND A GENUINE PASSION FOR EXPLORATION.

THIS BIOGRAPHY EXPLORES PALIN'S CONTRIBUTIONS TO COMEDY, HIS PIVOTAL ROLE IN THE GROUNDBREAKING MONTY PYTHON COMEDY SERIES, AND HIS EVOLUTION AS AN ACTOR AND WRITER. IT NAVIGATES THROUGH THE HIGHS AND LOWS OF HIS CAREER, SHEDDING LIGHT ON HIS COLLABORATIONS WITH COMEDY LEGENDS AND HIS SOLO VENTURES IN FILM AND TELEVISION.

THE NARRATIVE TAKES READERS BEHIND THE SCENES OF PALIN'S ACCLAIMED TRAVEL DOCUMENTARIES, UNVEILING THE INSPIRATIONS AND CHALLENGES HE ENCOUNTERED WHILE CIRCLING THE GLOBE. AS AN AVID EXPLORER, THE BIOGRAPHY CAPTURES THE ESSENCE OF PALIN'S WANDERLUST AND THE CULTURAL INSIGHTS HE GAINED FROM HIS JOURNEYS TO DIVERSE CORNERS OF THE WORLD.

WITH A KEEN FOCUS ON PALIN'S PERSONAL LIFE, INCLUDING HIS ENDURING MARRIAGE, FAMILY, AND PHILANTHROPIC ENDEAVORS, THE BIOGRAPHY PROVIDES A COMPREHENSIVE PORTRAIT OF THE MAN BEHIND THE LAUGHTER AND ADVENTURE. FROM ACCOLADES AND HONORS TO HIS IMPACT ON GEOGRAPHY EDUCATION, THE BOOK CELEBRATES MICHAEL PALIN'S LASTING LEGACY AND THE INDELIBLE MARK HE HAS LEFT ON THE REALMS OF COMEDY, TRAVEL, AND CULTURE.

ISBN 9798870318745

9 798870 318745

9 0 0 0